Great Yarmouth

IN OLD PHOTOGRAPHS

Cross Row, *c.* 1867. This row ran from midway down the south side of Row 1, in a north–south direction, cutting Row 2 in half, and on to the west end of Row 3. Cross Row was one of the few north–south passages, and was unnumbered. Most of the rows were paved with pebbles from the beach, which made walking anything but a pleasure. Later, as seen in this photograph, bricks were introduced.

Great Yarmouth

IN OLD PHOTOGRAPHS

MICHAEL TEUN

Alan Sutton Publishing Limited
Phoenix Mill · Far Thrupp · Stroud
Gloucestershire

First published 1994

Reprinted 1995

Copyright © Michael Teun, 1994

British Library Cataloguing in Publication Data.
A catalogue record for this book is available from
the British Library.

ISBN 0-7509-0755-X

Typeset in 9/10 Sabon.
Typesetting and origination by
Alan Sutton Publishing Limited.
Printed in Great Britain by
WBC Ltd, Bridgend, Mid-Glamorgan.

Contents

Introduction

Since medieval times, the lives of kings, vagabonds, artists, authors, poets and peasants have all been part of Great Yarmouth; their history and stories are imprinted on the ancient walls and buildings of the town. It is connected with many famous people: Admiral Lord Horatio Nelson, Sir James Paget, Anna Sewell, author of *Black Beauty*, Sarah Martin, the prison reformer, Lady Hamilton . . . the list goes on. The stories of intrigue, mystery, adventure and the unusual would make countless best-selling books.

Great Yarmouth's unique rows were likened by Charles Dickens to the bars of a gridiron. He describes a row thus: 'A Row is a long, narrow lane or alley quite straight, or as nearly as may be, with houses on each side, both of which you can sometimes touch at once with the finger tips of each hand, by stretching out your arms to their full extent. Now and then the houses overhang, and even join above your head converting the row so far into a sort of tunnel or tubular passage. Many picturesque old bits of domestic architecture are to be found among the rows. In some rows there is little more than a blank wall for the double boundary. In others the houses retreat into tiny square courts where washing and clear starching was done.'

In Roman times this part of the coast was a large estuary over 2 miles wide, which discharged the fresh water of the rivers into the sea. Later, a long thin island of sand and shingle began to emerge, dividing the estuary into northern and southern channels. The northern channel became blocked, and the sandbank continued to grow southwards as a long spit. Local tradition states that the sandbank was first inhabited soon after AD1000. The town's origins are probably even earlier, for by the time of the great Domesday survey of 1086, Yarmouth was a small but well-established community.

It is likely that it was Gorleston fishermen who first used the sandbank during Anglo-Saxon times, as a convenient place to pull up their boats and spread out their nets during the fishing season. In time, it also proved convenient to sell their catches on the spot; and as merchants and traders visited the sandbank, a permanent settlement grew up.

The town plan was based on three main streets that curved in a north–south direction along the sandbank; the buildings between them were arranged in blocks, with the rows dividing them east to west. The first mention of our rows was in 1286, when the number of rows in each leet (or ward) was given, and we find a total of some 140 rows. From this, it can be stated that the rows were firmly established by this time.

This was an important period in the development of Yarmouth, for in 1285 the work of building the town wall had started. It was the town wall that probably helped maintain Yarmouth's medieval street layout right up to the Second World War.

Great Yarmouth's geographical position at the mouth of a river system, serving one of the richest regions in medieval England, close to the important trading area across the North Sea, and with a flourishing herring fishery, made it a major sea port from the early Middle Ages. Being such an important town it had to be protected, and in 1261 Henry III gave permission for the building of a town wall. Work was not completed until about 1400. The area enclosed by this structure was 133 acres.

This period of prosperity was to be followed by a series of disasters. The harbour exit became blocked and the plague killed almost two-thirds of the inhabitants in 1348. No doubt the close proximity to each other of the houses in the town's rows played an important part in the rapid spread of the disease.

The successful completion of the new haven in the sixteenth century brought new wealth from Dutch settlers and a revival of the herring industry. This contributed greatly to Yarmouth's renewed increasing prosperity, and more fine buildings were constructed in the town during the sixteenth and seventeenth centuries.

The late seventeenth century was, however, an unsettled period for the town. Trade suffered as a result of Dutch competition and the almost continuous wars with the Dutch, Spanish and French, and the after-effects of the English Civil War.

The eighteenth century saw a period of great prosperity particularly with the herring trade, and by its end Yarmouth had become a fashionable watering-place, although seaside holidays were unheard of until 1750, when Dr Russell published a pamphlet recommending sea water as a cure for almost anything. Yarmouth soon opened a bath house, later to become the Bath Hotel. But Yarmouth still remained essentially within its walls until the nineteenth century. Outside the walls were open 'Denes' for drying fishing nets, and there were three batteries mounted with cannons, ready to defend the town. Windmills were also a sight to be seen on the skyline.

Development outside the walls was restricted in the early part of the nineteenth century, to protect the livelihood of the town's shopkeepers. But this was soon to lapse, for the coming of the railways in the mid-1840s turned Yarmouth into a real seaside resort. Until that time the town had almost retained its medieval pattern inside the walled boundary, but Albert Square, Kimberley Terrace and an ornamental arch in Wellington Road were followed in the 1850s by the construction of Marine Parade and Drive. In 1854 the Wellington Pier was opened. A second, the Britannia Pier, opened four years later. Both still survive today. Meanwhile, terraced cottages were spreading outside the line of the old walls. In 1854 a new iron Haven Bridge had replaced the narrow wooden bridge, and this facilitated the growth of Southtown.

From the eighteenth century there were groups of beachmen who kept tall wooden lookouts on the beach and made a living from salvage. Later, many of these beachmen used their adapted boats to run pleasure trips from the beach.

By the end of the nineteenth century, there were three railway stations, Southtown, Beach and Vauxhall. Vauxhall, the oldest, and today the sole survivor, brought thousands of trippers to the town. Paddle-steamers arrived from the Thames estuary, and even seasickness did not prevent the visitors, once ashore, from the enjoyment of shrimp teas, or cockles, washed down with pints of Lacon's beer. Such was Victorian Yarmouth, whose character did not change much until the Second World War.

An old saying described Yarmouth as 'a town of pubs'. This remark was not particularly original, because much the same thing was said about other sizeable East Anglian towns. A visitor to Yarmouth around fifty years ago might have been justified in thinking that such was the case, because there was hardly a street or a road that did not have a public house, or so it seemed, every few yards.

Vast tracts of the original row area were destroyed by enemy action during the Second World War. So much of the history of the town was in these rows, and it is a great pity that some were not saved. The town can never be the same without them.

Unfortunately, the gradual elimination of private traders, with their quaint shop fronts, proved to be one of the penalties of progress. To our grandparents, the back-streets were important places, associated for many generations with cabinet-makers, clock-makers, bakers and many other trades. These shops opened at all hours, and even at midnight the old traders would have been reluctant to close their doors. In streets like Middlegate many of these shops were found on the corners of the rows.

The photographers of the day, who set up their cameras and recorded the old shops and pubs, left the legacy that enables future generations to see what our old town was like in bygone days. Without these dedicated men, publications like this would never have been possible. So it is to these people we must render our thanks.

SECTION ONE

The Rows

Blyth's Tobacconists, Broad Row. One of the more striking figures, impossible to miss in Yarmouth, was a strapping great Highlander that stood in the entrance of Blyth's Tobacconists at 17/18 Broad Row. The figure already stood there, like the guardian of the row, when Robert Blyth purchased the business in around 1850. He was still on parade when the shop was bought out by another Broad Row tobacconists, Nortons, just before the Second World War. Shortly before the shop closed in the early 1970s the figure was sold to a snuff manufacturer in Sheffield, who maintains a museum of such trade signs.

A Yarmouth row, *c.* 1867. Most histories give this as Row 2, but it is more likely to be Row 23. Note the open gutter running down the side: the open gutters of the rows accumulated a great deal of filth, which must have encouraged the spread of disease. The rows were so narrow in places that people on one side could shake hands from their windows with people on the other.

Row 23, showing the Auxiliary Fire Service during the Second World War. Most of the old Row 23 had been cleared because of pre-war slum clearance and wartime bombing.

Row 22, *c*. 1939. This row ran from the Market Place to Howard Street North, and its line can be seen on the left. The photograph shows the buildings between Rows 22 and 24 being demolished to extend the Conge through to the Market Place. The site of the row today forms the north pavement of the Conge, which originally ran only from the Quay to George Street.

Row 24, *c*. 1939. Another scene showing the Conge being extended through to the Market Place. The row now forms the southern pavement of the Conge.

Row 42, 1950s. For many years a synagogue stood in this row. The row on the left, which ran from George Street to Howard Street, can be seen, but the buildings in George Street have already been cleared.

From Palmer's in the Market Place looking out over roof-tops towards Row 60, 1950s. The Quaker Meeting House which still stands today is seen at the west end of this row, but most of the other buildings in this area were cleared to accommodate Palmer's car park.

Row 45, 1920s. On the left in the foreground we see George Perrin, a well-known chimney-sweep. This row ran from George Street to North Quay.

Row 54 was known locally as Palmer's Arcade, as it divided Palmer's shop. It was absorbed into the store in the 1960s.

Row 92, photographed around 1943, showing heavy bomb damage to a seventeenth-century row house. The night of 7/8 April 1941 saw the destruction of a large number of rows and properties in the Middlegate Street area. This turned out to be the worst raid of the war. Some 4,000 incendiary bombs were dropped on Great Yarmouth in one night, causing 65 major fires and nearly 200 smaller ones. The additional effect of parachute mines caused the almost total destruction of a considerable amount of property in the row area. Note the cistern still hanging from the wall, bottom right-hand side of the photograph.

Row 60, Howard Street South to King Street, before the Second World War. In 1884 a start was made on concreting these footpaths. At the time of these improvements, an official measure of eighty-one of the rows was taken, and their total length was ascertained at 8,372 yd, or rather more than 4½ miles. The entire length of all the rows exceeded 7 miles.

Row 95, or 'Kitty Witches Row', 1920s. The western end of this row was only 24 in wide. In Yarmouth the term Kitty Witch was applied to women with blood-smeared faces who, fantastically dressed, paraded the town demanding contributions at certain seasons of the year.

Row 99, 'Castle Row', 1860s. A castle in the immediate vicinity of this row was described by the Yarmouth historian Manship as 'seated in the midst of the town, a castle or military forefence'. It was a square building with a watch-tower at each corner. The top of the castle was taken down in 1620 and the castle yard was finally sold to Thomas Penrice. He built coach-houses and stables on the site, which later became the Penrice Arms. Row 99 ran from Middlegate Street to King Street.

Row 116, Middlegate Street to King Street, 1920s. At the far end of this row in Middlegate Street can be seen the Druids Arms, and next door to that was the rag-and-bone shop of Horace Butcher who was murdered in 1934. It was in this row that he was last seen alive as he walked home.

Row 116, 1935. A row party to celebrate the Silver Jubilee of George V. This was probably one of many held in this row, which would have been closed at each end for the event.

Unfortunately the number of this row is not known. Vast areas of these unique rows were destroyed by enemy action during the last war.

Row 120, with one side awaiting demolition, 1950s. A sad ending to one of old Yarmouth's rows.

The same row. The whole family posing for the photograph in happier days between the wars.

Brenner's Bazaar, 1931. Staff pose outside their Yarmouth Market Row and Howard Street North corner premises. Miss Ethel Howell and Miss Gladys Wells are on either side of the men in the doorway. The bazaar closed in the late 1930s, and later became Peacock's.

Row 142, looking west towards the Quay. There were 145 numbered rows, but there were several short rows with numbers such as 51½, 34½ and 91½. There were other rows, for example Broad Row and Market Row, that were never numbered at all. As many as 156 rows were recorded at one time.

Part of the row area in Middlegate Street was taken over for training purposes during the Second World War. Both of these photographs show a rescue being made from the row house which had already been bombed.

The Broad Row, looking west, 1922. Stead & Simpson's shoe and boot shops are on both sides of the row, and at numbers 17/18 on the left our Scotsman figure can be seen standing in the entrance of Blyth's. On the right-hand side brushes are hanging outside Arthur Ellis's shop. Ellis was one of Yarmouth's last brushmakers.

The Broad Row, looking east, 1922. Middleton's newsagent was on the left-hand side, next door to Boots the Chemists who opened in the row in 1896. Platten's can be seen on the same side. Opposite on the corner is Sullivan's sweet shop; and Middleton's smaller second shop was next door to Sullivan's.

SECTION TWO

Market Place

Market Place, late 1880s. The Market Place is an open plain of about 3½ acres, but had originally been much larger, for it encompassed the entire area from the buildings on the west side to the town wall. All signs of the pillory or stretch neck, the stocks and the cage in which vagrants and disorderly persons were held, have long since vanished. In 1546 the town built a large building for the use of country butchers, and in 1551, the butchery proving a success, slaughterhouses were built on the east side of the Market Place, and all meat was ordered to be sold here.

Market Place, 1870s. The buildings to the right, 1 and 2 Market Place, were known to locals as 'Burroughs' Corner', the name being derived from William Burroughs, wine merchant, who purchased 2 Market Place in 1812. The shop with the extended blind, no. 4, was at this time owned by Mr Thomas George, a newsagent, but by the turn of the century his business had been taken over by Middleton's. One of the Market Place water pumps which stood opposite the corner of today's Conge is to the left.

Leach's hardware shop at 20 Market Place. This business was established in Yarmouth in 1868. Note the price of a bath-tub.

Market Place, 1864. Most of the shops on the east side were butchers as a result of the very early order to sell meat here and nowhere else under penalty of a 20-shilling fine. The Fish Market, almost across what today is Middlemarket Road, is seen to the right.

The Fish Market, 1864. It was roofed over in 1625. In 1844 a new market was formed, surrounded by iron balustrades, which lasted until its demolition in 1869. On the other side of Middlemarket Road was one of Yarmouth's many public houses, the Bull.

A motor-bike rally in the late 1950s. The building work going on in this scene is for a new Woolworths store, dating this photograph to 1958.

Looking down the east side of the Market Place, before 1910. A gentleman riding a penny-farthing bike can be picked out from among the carts going about their business.

Elmo Food Fare, which was found in the 1960s at no. 18 Market Place. It was one of Yarmouth's first self-service stores.

The interior of Elmo's store. Note the prices.

Many a Yarmouth man used to drop into the Two Necked Swan for a pint of 'river water' before the Second World War. The dregs of every bottle went into a glass barrel to form the potent brew, and its name came from the sludge at the bottom. It sold at a shilling a glass and never tasted the same twice.

Nos 4 to 8 Market Place, during the Second World War. From right to left, bomb damage can be seen on the gable end of Middleton's, the newsagents. Next door is Steward's chemist's shop. The Two Necked Swan, with the landlord's name displayed above, is at no. 6. A small boot shop next to that was owned in the 1930s by Mr Richardson; this today is part of the Two Necked Swan. Just seen to the far left is William Barnes' grocer's

McCarthy shops on the east side of the Market Place, 1950s. The confectionery sign above no. 55 was from an earlier trader, Mr Skoyles. On this side of the Market Place all the earlier mentioned butchers' shops had evidently changed to fruiterers by this time.

Gray's market stall at about 7.30 a.m. on a Saturday in 1921. The price of rump steak is only 1s a pound. On the right is Mr Walter Sayer and on the left is Mr Joe Bunn.

The stalls on the Market Place, 1880s. Wednesdays and Saturdays have been market days for many years. Countrymen bring in the choice produce of the neighbouring agricultural district.

Mrs Majorie Smedley outside the Two Necked Swan. Bert Smedley, who ran this public house for many years, died in 1952, and his widow, Marjorie, with the help of their daughter, took over the licence. They had to retire the following year, after thirty years' service behind the bar.

Mr Smedley's delivery van parked outside his pub in the late 1920s.

The Red House. A feature of this pub was a model railway built by the landlord, Mr Moore, in 1939. The train could be worked by any member of the public by the insertion of a coin in a slot.

Mr Moore seen attending to his railway which was over 70 ft long. It encircled the room of his bar on a wide ledge near the top of the walls.

East side of the Market Place, between 1883 and 1887. From left to right, a water cart is taking on water outside Southey's, the saddler. Next door is the butcher's shop of William Christmas. A drink could be had at the Duke of Sussex public house, and following on to no. 58, a meal could be bought from Thompson's eating house. Before we reach the Bull public house, Mr Swann, Mr Bunn and Christopher Bales (butchers) all make up 'The Butchery', as local people once called this side of the Market Place.

Cattle passing the Co-op store in the Market Place, almost certainly on their way to the slaughterhouse, probably in the 1950s.

The Central cinema opened on Easter Monday, 5 April 1915. It stood on the site of the Bijou Hall, which was described (in 1913) as assembly rooms. The Central was renamed the Plaza in 1928. During the Second World War after Marks & Spencer's King Street premises were destroyed by bombing, the seating was removed, and it was used as temporary premises. The building never again operated as a cinema. Palmer's also used it in 1953 to store customers' flood-damaged furniture. In 1958 the Plaza was finally demolished and a new store for Woolworths was built on the site (see page 26).

Samuel Randell's shop at 41/42 Market Place in the 1890s. Mr Randell came to Yarmouth in 1860 in search of work with only one shilling in his pocket after two years as a journeyman. By 1862 he had opened his first shop at 63a Market Place. After a further move to Market Row by 1882, he had purchased no. 42 and a few years later expanded into 41 Market Place.

By the late 1920s the premises at 41/42 Market Place were occupied by Palmer's menswear shop. The old roof line of Mr Randell's shop can still be seen.

Palmer's department store has dominated the Market Place for well over 150 years. Garwood Palmer opened his first shop at 39 Market Place in 1837. By the time this photograph was taken in 1874 it was still only a double-fronted shop.

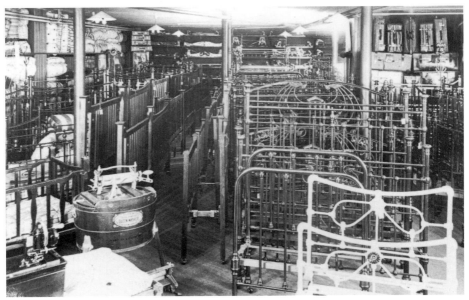

The interior of Palmer's in 1907 showing the furniture department. Note the washing machine.

SECTION THREE

Quayside

The Town Hall, completed in 1716, seen here in the early 1880s. By the beginning of the eighteenth century, the old guild hall at the church gate was falling into decay. The Corporation decided to erect a spacious new hall in a more central position, and for this purpose selected a site on the Quay. In 1842 a police court, station house and detention cells were built adjoining the Town Hall at the north-east corner. The clock was added in 1862 and was sold in 1889 for £1 16s. The grand front of this building faced the river.

Hall Quay, just before the turn of the century. In 1882 a new Town Hall was built overlapping the site of the demolished 1716 Town Hall. It was opened by the Prince of Wales, with 350 guests invited to lunch and a grand firework display on the Britannia Pier in the evening. Note the horse bus at the foot of the bridge.

The Town Hall that dominated the quayside became the Council's greatest worry in 1886. The hall developed trouble when the building settled towards the river, when it had only been standing for four years. The Council even discussed pulling it down, as large cracks appeared on the west and north sides. The solution was finally found by an engineer, Mr Duckham, with the use of screw piles. The hall is pictured in 1887.

The west side of the Town Hall, in 1887, showing the screw piles and wrought-iron girders which supported the whole western portion of the block. By a gradual screwing up of each pile the building was raised.

South Quay looking north, with the old Town Hall on the right, 1870s. With the ships moored along the quayside and the children looking on, it is a remarkably peaceful sight.

South Quay, 1870s. In 1724 Defoe said of Yarmouth that 'It had the finest quay in England if not in Europe'. Sadly today the line of trees has gone and the carriage has been replaced by a continuous stream of motor traffic.

Hall Quay, before 1871. The coach is standing outside the Duke's Head. It was from this inn that the London stage-coach set out when it was first established in the second half of the seventeenth century. Next door to the Duke's Head is a public house called The Barge. The end of George Street is seen with a private house on the left, which today is Mr Malcolm Ferrow's antiques shop.

The Bell & Crown stood on the north-west corner of Row 133 facing South Quay. It seems that almost every Yarmouth row had a public house on one of its corners.

The Upper Ferry Inn stood on the south-west corner of Row 136 facing South Quay. Except for the ground floor, which is boxed out, this building had changed little since it was built early in the seventeenth century.

The Haven Bridge and Hall Quay, *c.* 1876. The bridge was opened in 1854. The building under construction on Hall Quay is a new shop for Mr John Clowes, a grocer. The tall bay-fronted house to the right was the home of Lady Orde, which was soon to be demolished, and the present day Star and Garter built on the site. The old Star and Garter shown next to Lady Orde's house was pulled down to extend the then Lacon, Youell Bank which today is Lloyds Bank.

Post office, Hall Quay, 1860s. Yarmouth's first post office was in Row 107. By 1836 the office had moved to Row 63. With a need for larger premises a further move was made to Hall Quay in 1840. The final move to the old Corn Hall, Regent Street, was in 1871, and this is where we find, much extended, today's post office.

Haven Bridge, *c*. 1852. A very early Yarmouth photograph which can be dated by two buildings and the bridge. The wooden bridge shown was erected as a temporary bridge in 1836, at a cost of £1,465; it was intended to last ten years. In fact it survived eighteen years, until 1854, when it was replaced. The bank at the foot of the bridge was rebuilt in 1854 too, and the Star and Garter, with its smooth square-cut flintstone dressing, was bricked up in the same year. The photograph shows all three before the alterations.

SECTION FOUR

Streets

Gaol Street, 1860s. The Yarmouth gaol was closed in 1875 and the buildings were used as a remand centre until 1877. The building to the rear of the old Tolhouse (newer part of the gaol) was demolished in 1883, and the new library now stands on the site. After 1875 Gaol Street was renamed Middlegate Street. The building with the sign and a lady standing in the doorway is a tavern called the Cock, whose name was later changed to the Middlegate Tavern. In 1863 the double bay-fronted shop two doors away was owned by Samuel Bowles, a rag dealer. In 1874 the taller building between these two was owned by William Neslen, a ginger-beer maker.

Middlegate Street, 1920s. On the left Mr La'Porte's shop at nos 88 and 89 is just in view. After his death Mrs La'Porte took over the business. The shop opened all hours and sold everything. The end of Row 144 is seen next. The sunlight is shining out of Row 143.

Middlegate Street, 1943. The tall building to the far left is no. 41; next door is Jary's butcher's shop. Two doors away we find the famous barber of Middlegate Street, Henry Davis. The west end of Row 120 and the bombed shop of tailor Herbert Moore are then passed, with the end of Row 121 to the far right.

Middlegate Street. The demolition of the old Middlegate Street started in the early 1950s.

No. 63 Middlegate Street, Mr Charles Claxton's fishmonger's shop.

The Magdala Tavern is on the left of Row 124. To the right at 140 Middlegate Street are the premises of basket-maker Mr Sharman. This photograph was taken in the 1920s.

Regent Street, looking east, late 1870s. The post office is on the left. Regent Street was opened in 1813 to relieve traffic that passed through the Broad Row and Market Row, and also to give a wider thoroughfare from the Quay to King Street. A condition was made that no shop or public house could be erected in the new street.

Regent Street, 1870s. The gentleman standing near the lamp-post looks like an early policeman with his top hat. Opposite, on the corner of 'Blind Howard Street', as locals called it, can be seen a chemist's sign. For many years Valentine Cross traded here, and Boots took over the premises in 1894. This was their first shop in Yarmouth.

Hunts' ginger-beer factory in Howard Street South. The factory was cleared in the 1960s to make way for Palmer's car park.

'Blind Howard Street', looking towards Regent Street, c. 1925. Locals gave this part of Howard Street the name because it came to an abrupt end at Row 90. In the background work is going on to demolish Row 74 and others, to build the present-day arcade.

Howard Street South, 1950s. On the corner of Row 56 was a large house called Selbourne House. In 1845 the Yarmouth Savings Bank moved from Row 66 to this house, moving again to the Market Place in 1859. The gable end of Downing's, a baker, with the end of Row 54, is to the far left. The site today is Palmer's car park.

George Street: a carefree group of children in the 1950s. The photograph shows David Newman, Patrick and Graham Connett playing in a clearance area opposite the Broad Row.

A party in progress near the electricity sub-station on the west side of George Street, 1930s. It is not known whether these coronation celebrations were for Edward VIII or George VI.

George Street, looking from Fullers Hill, late 1920s. Many large seventeenth-century houses were found in this street. Originally George Street was called Northgate, not to be confused with the later street named after the gate outside the town wall. Some early documents refer to the street as Conge Street.

Mrs Thompson, a well-known and much-remembered character of George Street, standing outside her house at no. 46.

The Wheel of Fortune public house, much frequented by the local residents of George Street in the 1920s. The pub stood on the corner of Row 30.

King Street, looking towards the Market Place, late 1850s. A soldier in full dress uniform is to the left, and a few yards towards the Market Place is the junction of Regent Street and King Street. The shop on the corner with the sun blinds is Mr Dendy's, a draper's shop. His name can just be seen above. Next door was a grocer, William Tuttle, with William Alexander, bookseller, at no. 180. This old shop can be picked out by the large square window of the upper storey. Mr Alexander died in 1858 and his business was sold in 1860 to another bookseller, William Burton, who rebuilt the premises.

Looking towards the junction of Regent Street and King Street, 1860s. Just in view to the right is Bond's chemist's shop with the end of Row 63 to the left. George Nall's bookshop is on the other side of the row. The next building is the old Shakespeare Tavern, which by this time had been converted into a toy shop for Sarah Carrell. The rebuilt shop of 1860 was then owned by John Cossons, draper, who in 1869 sold out to Frank and William Arnold. This was the birth of the later large department store. Mr Tuttle is still trading but the corner site sees the shop of Mr Thomas George, another draper.

From 181 King Street looking towards the Market Place, *c.* 1867. Just visible to the left is the old Shakespeare Tavern, followed by Mr Nall's bookshop. The sign above Mr Bond's chemist shop (who died in 1868) can be seen next door. Another bookseller, Mr Norman, is at no. 184, with yet another public house, The Oxford, coming next. John Parson's draper's shop at 42 Market Place, with the sun blinds over the window, leads us into the Market Place. Palmer's can be seen with the steps outside. To the left of Palmer's is The Elephant and Castle public house, which much later became The Red House.

Miller's Royal Studios, 14 King Street, in the 1890s. By the turn of the century Mrs Miller had converted the building to the left into a shop, and moved there. Tom Green had taken over the corner shop which gave the corner its name. It is still referred to by locals as 'Tom Green's corner'.

Arnold's shop, 1897. The middle bay is the original shop and by this time the shops on either side had been purchased. Row 66 can just be seen to the left.

Mr Nall's bookshop, 182 King Street, 1860s. There has been a bookshop on this site since at least 1813, when it was first opened by Charles Sloman. Sloman retired in 1857 and George Nall took over. Well over a hundred years ago, on 1 May 1888, the present proprietors, Jarrolds, purchased Nall's old shop and printing works in Row 63.

King Street, looking north. Before the turn of the century this historic road was a main shopping street.

King Street, before 1902. The horse and cart is about to turn down Regent Road with Divers public house on the far corner.

A carnival procession in King Street in the 1920s.

SECTION FIVE

Entertainment and Recreation

Theatre Royal, Regent Road. The photograph shows the rear of the theatre with shops facing Regent Road, the front being on Theatre Plain. It was built by Scott & Harrison of Yarmouth for a cost of £1,500 and took eight months to build, opening in 1778. Improvements were made in 1820 and 1828.

The Regal was built on the site of the former Theatre Royal. Redevelopment of the old theatre had been in the news since 1929. Plans were passed by the local council, but the scheme collapsed when the original builder went bankrupt. The cinema was finally built by J. Balls & Sons of Yarmouth.

The Regal under construction. The whole auditorium and front entrance block was steel framed, with some of the upright girders weighing 9 tons.

The Regal, a £50,000 monument to local enterprise, opened on 1 January 1934.

The Regal during construction. The site was long and narrow and the stipulation for seating capacity of 1,500 resulted in a lofty auditorium with a steep balcony.

Fair time in Yarmouth Market Place. The oyster stall is to the left.

Bathers at Yarmouth, 1920s.

The Marina, 1950s. Built on the site of the Singers Ring and opened in 1937, it was demolished in 1978 and today's Marina Leisure Centre was built on the site.

The Circus. A Mr George Gilbert had been promoting circus performances in Norwich. Finding these to be successful, he then erected a circus building in Yarmouth on the site of the Bath Hotel stables, St George's Road, which opened in 1898. The venture was so successful that he decided to erect the present Hippodrome which opened to the public in July 1903.

The Regent was equipped for film and stage shows, and styled on a West End theatre. It was said to be like the London Coliseum when it opened in 1914. The Regent still stands proudly today, but stripped of most of its former glory.

The Aquarium, late 1870s. The Aquarium was built on the site of one of the town batteries at the northern end of the Marine Parade. It was equipped with eighteen fish tanks up to 50 ft in length. A skating rink was built on the flat roof of the aquarium. The opening ceremony was held on 5 September 1876 and the roller-skating rink opened in February 1877. The stairs to the skating rink can be seen on the left of the building. A bandstand is also visible to the rear of the rink.

The Royal Aquarium was renamed after one of several visits by the Prince of Wales, and is pictured here after 1897. The Aquarium was rebuilt with an upper storey in 1883 and there is a date-stone on the building with this date.

Bathers on Yarmouth beach, 1898.

Paddling at Yarmouth, 1898.

Hotchkiss' Railway, opened in 1895, had four to six machines on each track which made a circle of about 250 ft. This ride, together with another American ride, the Switchback, was situated on the west side of North Drive. As the building line crept northwards along North Drive, the machines moved with it, until the final move between Beaconsfield and Salisbury Road. There it remained until 1909 when it was removed to Yorkshire.

A tram passing the Jetty. The strollers on the Marine Parade look very decorous. The tramway opened in Yarmouth in 1902.

Ansel Place. These buildings were reputed to have been the first to be used as lodging houses. Seaside holidays were unheard of until the middle of the eighteenth century, when Dr Russell published a pamphlet recommending sea water as a universal cure. Yarmouth soon took advantage of the new fashion of bathing in salt water, and in 1759 a bath house was opened which later became the Bath Hotel. By the 1820s the more hardy were bathing in the open sea. Ansel Place was demolished, and in 1911 the Empire cinema was built on part of the site.

A scene from around 1867 showing fishermen and beachmen listening to a lady playing the harp while seated on the Jetty.

Marine Parade, 1922. In the foreground the swimming pool which opened on 22 July 1922 is under construction. The Royal Aquarium and the revolving tower are in the background.

This is the original entrance to Yarmouth's Pleasure Beach, a meccano-style gantry straddling the entrance, in the 1920s. The showman in the early days of the Pleasure Beach was Mr Pat Collins. In 1954 Albert and James Botton took over the park.

The Pleasure Beach, showing the ark, which was constructed in 1925, and made of steel and wood covered in plasterwork. This was the scene of a fire in 1932.

Britannia Pier was built in 1858 at the northern end of Marine Parade. It has had a very chequered career. Twice cut in half by ships (in 1859 and 1868), its pavilions were destroyed by fire in 1909, 1914 and 1954. The photograph shows the pier before the turn of the century.

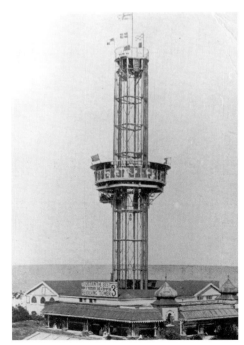

The revolving tower was built in 1897 by Thomas Warwick. The foundations for this tower were 8 ft thick, and filled with 350 tons of concrete. The tower was demolished for scrap in 1941.

All the fun of Yarmouth's Easter Fair on Church Plain, 1890s.

SECTION SIX

Shop Fronts
and
Public Houses

Maypole Dairy shops were found in almost every town of any size throughout the country. Their style of shop front was universal, and it is impossible to identify any particular shop without some local knowledge. This shop was in the Broad Row. Maypole also had a branch in King Street and one in Gorleston High Street.

Brett's shop on Church Plain, seen here with its fleet of vans outside, before the Second World War. Brett's was established in Yarmouth in 1892. The Church Plain premises were badly damaged during the war and later had to be pulled down.

Brett's Market Row premises where the same family trades today.

Downing's Arcade Stores at 9 Howard Street South, seen just before the shop was demolished in the 1960s. The site today forms part of Palmer's car park.

Mr Lambert's Tea Shop in the Broad Row, *c.* 1900. The tempting aroma of tea and coffee was a feature of this shop.

Here is Mr Percy Read standing with a delivery boy in the doorway of his shop at 27 Howard Street North. This business was first established in 1844, selling butter, eggs, homemade lard, pickles, cooked pies, home cured hams and last but not least the noble sausage. Mr Read was a real favourite with the row population with his many lines in meat.

No. 5 Howard Street North. This was Pagano's fruit shop in the 1920s.

Southgate's butcher's shop, 21 Howard Street North. Row 38 can be seen to the left. Mr Southgate's shop was on the east side, where Yarmouth's police station is found today.

Mr Edwards' shellfish shop at 79 Howard Street South. Pink shrimps could be bought for 1*d* a pint while brown were 2*d* a pint. This old shop was trading until the late 1960s; it was eventually demolished in the early 1970s. One of the features of this shop was its early nineteenth-century shop front, saved from demolition by Malcolm Ferrow. He has kept it in storage to this day.

The premises of Mr Syd Clarke, a very popular hairdresser in Howard Street South. Like most Yarmouth barbers he always had a tale to tell.

Syd Clarke inside his shop, just about to say 'Who's next for a short back and sides?'

Mr Blagg's grocer's shop is to the left and Tom Green, outfitter, is next door. Tom Green had three shops in King Street at this time (1910): the one shown, no. 19 and his corner premises, no. 14.

Walter Bebee,'s premises, King Street, 1910. This old shop with a bakery to the rear was situated on the corner of Row 113. The shop today belongs to Peter Howkins, antiques dealer.

Frogs Hall Curing Works in South Market Road. Mr Colby was the fish merchant who gave the building its name. The clock is the one from the old Town Hall which was sold in 1889 for £1 16s. The Co-op later demolished this building and built a warehouse on the site. The clock finished up on the Co-op's other premises in Middle Market Road.

Mr Mays' butcher's shop, 56 Middlegate Street, with the window decorated for Christmas. Almost every type of joint of meat can be seen hanging ready to be sold.

Mitchell's fish shop, 114 Middlegate Street, in the 1930s. In the window to the left a print of a cat is seen glazed into the tiles.

Halls' butcher's shop at 123 King Street on the corner of Row 122, 1910. Halls had two shops in Yarmouth between the wars, the other situated in Nelson Road. The family were well known for their shops and friendly service. As the photograph demonstrates Halls always had a good display of meat.

Lacon's Brewery gate, Church Plain. A significant feature of this brewery were the many tablets affixed to the buildings, setting the year of erection. The entrance, and gateway displaying the falcon, was erected in 1868. The chestnut tree was an object of interest in the centre of the yard. Sadly this once-great brewery closed a few years later, after merging with Whitbreads in 1966.

Lacon's Brewery viewed from St Nicholas's Church tower.

The York public house in King Street, one of Yarmouth's numerous pubs. It is pictured in the 1920s.

The Earl St Vincent public house, 93 King Street, was formerly called the White Swan. Row 140 is to the right.

The Falcon, North Quay, pictured around 1925, with Row 28 to the left. Continuing along North Quay, we can see Mr Harwood's barber's shop followed by Self's Garage, with its sign above. Later on Self's took over the complete site and turned the ground floor of the old Falcon into a car showroom.

The North Star public house on the corner of Fullers Hill, *c.* 1922. The west end of Row 9 is to the left.

Quay Mill Tavern, North Quay, c. 1922. As with many of these public houses it changed its name with the coming of the railways. This pub became The Railway Hotel; but in later years the name reverted back to the Quay Mill.

The New Queen's Head, 83 Howard Street South, with Row 50 to the left, 1920s. There was hardly a street or road, however short, which did not have some famous arms, a bygone hero or the name of a forgotten battle depicted on the sign above its public house.

The Queen's Head, 16 Howard Street North, *c*. 1922. To confuse the researcher there were two public houses in Howard Street with almost the same name. This pub stood between Row 29 to the left and Row 32 to the right. Mr Darn's fish shop can just be seen to the far right.

The Gallon Pot, 42 Howard Street North, late 1920s. The site of this pub today is the east end of St Francis Way. The small bars in these pubs were made snug and warm in winter by a coal fire.

The Vine, between Row 49 and Row 51 in Howard Street South, 1920s. The site today is the roadway to the north of Palmer's car park.

The Rose and Crown, 45 Howard Street North, *c.* 1922. In pre-war days, redundancy was the fate that hung over the heads of quite a few of these pubs at the annual licensing sessions. Although they put up a stout battle to survive, some, like this pub, lost. In the 1930s this old public house became a dairy. Row 41 is seen to the left.

The Army and Navy on Blackfriars Road, with Tudman's hardware shop next door, *c.* 1922. Another public house, The Blackfriars Tavern, is to the far right.

The Sailor's Return. The location is unknown, but the photograph was taken around 1920.

The New Fountain Tavern, 127 Middlegate Street, 1920s. Row 136 is to the left. This public house is known to have been rebuilt in the 1870s.

The Fishing Boat, 111 Middlegate Street, c. 1925. The fishermen regularly consumed a large amount of beer. Apparently the local boats were supplied with quantities of beer for their voyages, and there was then scope for the small old-fashioned brewhouses that were once found in the rows.

The Turk's Head, 1920s. It stood on the south-east corner of Row 96, fronting on Middlegate Street. A new façade to the pub was built in the 1870s. This pub was formerly called The Town Arms and afterwards The White Bear.

The Suffolk Tavern, 166 Middlegate Street, c. 1922. The wall of the Salvation Army building, which still stands today, can be seen to the left, with Row 103 to the right.

The Yarmouth Fishery, 1920s. This was one of the many pubs to be found in Middlegate Street, and stood on the corner of Friars Lane and Middlegate Street.

The Barking Smack public house on Marine Parade has a date-stone from 1845. John Day was the landlord at that time.

Arnold's furniture shop on the corner of the Market Row and Howard Street before the turn of the century.

Edward Harrison's grocer's shop, Market Row, facing the Market Place in the 1880s. The east end of the Market Row at this time was much narrower and built over. A grocer's shop stood on this site from at least 1790 with Barker and Fenn grocers, until the International Stores closed in the late 1960s.

SECTION SEVEN
Fires and Floods

Arnold's fire, 4 February 1919. Fire broke out in Arnold's block of drapery buildings facing King Street, and in an incredibly short time the whole building was alight. There was one vast sheet of searing flame stretching from King Street almost to Howard Street. The fire had such power that before long it began to travel down Regent Street, engulfing further shops as it spread.

Arnold's corner, showing the tower which was built in 1905, and the store, completely gutted by the fire. The store was rebuilt, and the chance to expand was taken with the purchase of the neighbouring burnt-out shops in Regent Street.

The Britannia Pier has been dogged by disaster. Its pavilions were destroyed by fire in 1909, 1914 and again in 1954. Here the pavilion is shown well alight in 1909, with crowds of onlookers on the beach. The cause of the fire was uncertain, but at one point a fused electric light bulb was blamed.

Another scene of a Britannia Pier fire. The suffragettes were blamed for the 1914 fire. Pieces of burning material were picked up at the far end of Regent Road near to the Regal. The pavilions stood no chance of surviving, as they were made largely of wood.

The scene after the Winton's Rooms or Goode's Hotel fire, on 5 September 1901. The fire had started in the hairdressing shop next door. A passer-by broke down the door after seeing smoke, just before the whole place burst into flames.

Builders ready to repair Goode's Hotel after the fire. A grand hotel rose from the ashes of the old building, where couples once waltzed on one of the finest dance floors in East Anglia. Sadly today only the upper façade remains, the building being used as an amusement arcade.

Palmer's fire in the Market Place in 1892. The fire started in the early hours of one morning just before Christmas and raged for a further six hours. The damage to the store and stock was estimated at more than £10,000.

Palmer's fire, 1892. The twenty workers who lived on the premises ran to the new shop, which escaped most of the fire because of a thick wall. A few months before the fire Palmer's had acquired 37 Market Place to expand.

The Cliff Hotel was destroyed by fire on Boxing Day, 1915. It was impossible to save the building because of a furious westerly gale that raged during that night and through to the early hours of the next day. The damage amounted to between £50,000 and £60,000.

Johnson's factory fire on Admiralty Road with crowds of onlookers.

One of Yarmouth's worst fires, with three acres of woodyard and timber alight, 1913. The heat of the blaze was scorching. As this photograph shows, the man with the hose has a blanket over his head. The fire-fighters remained on the scene for twenty-four hours.

The floods on North Quay, 1953. The new bridge can be seen with the old one by its side ready to be demolished.

The floods on North Quay, 1905. From right to left, Delf's grocer's premises are shown with the group of people standing outside; next door is the North Tower public house, and the Norwich Arms. The opening is Rainbow Corner.

SECTION EIGHT

Miscellany

This 1847 bridge over the Bure replaced the earlier suspension bridge, which had collapsed in May 1845 killing seventy-nine people. This happened when a clown was being towed up the river by four geese. As all the people who were watching the event moved from one side of the bridge to the other, to see the clown pass underneath, a weld gave way. Many fell to their death into the water. The photograph, taken in the late 1860s, looks west, with the toll-house on the right-hand side.

Church Plain, 1870s. Today, the private house to the left is a shop. The cart is standing alongside a water-pump, possibly taking on water.

Early days of St George's Park, which was laid out by the corporation in 1866. Last's windmill is in the background, with the Baptist Chapel to the left.

A refreshment cart at the fish-wharf.

A ginger-beer seller on North Quay, c. 1867. The houses on the other side of the road were just past the Conge, where later Johnson's clothing factory was built.

Looking from the Britannia Pier towards Regent Road in the 1870s. James Last's windmill, north of Albion Road, is to the left. The small group of buildings to the left of Regent Road is part of the old Mill House, from the remains of Pilch's windmill. The last mention of this mill was in 1850, and soon after this it was demolished. By 1854 the old Mill House had been purchased by Edward Steward for a summer residence. In 1874 the house was demolished and later the Queen's Hotel, which opened in 1885, was built on the site.

North Quay, 1880s. The White Swan public house is to the right and the cottages between the north-west tower (part of the town wall) and the river were sold in 1894 and later demolished.

Regent Road, looking towards King Street, early 1870s. The large building on the corner is Dean House. Today, a Kentucky Fried Chicken takeaway stands on the site. The name Flower can be read on the wooden building to the right. A fruiterer by that name was trading further down the road in the late 1860s, and possibly used this building as a store.

Regent Road, looking east, 1870s. Dene House is just seen to the right. When this photograph was taken, Regent Road was mainly residential.

Town Wall House, Regent Road, pictured in the 1920s, shortly before its demolition. The Electric House was built on the site.

The Electric House, Regent Road, which opened in 1929. The Regal is also seen in the background.

The Queen's Hotel, Regent Road, on the corner of Apsley Road, 1870s. By 1888 the hotel had closed and the building had become a girls' school. The landlord of the old Queen's was then found at the newly built Queen's Hotel on the corner of Regent Road and Marine Parade. Just after the turn of the century Jarrold's converted the building into a shop.

Salisbury Road. The buildings are yet to pass the railway line.

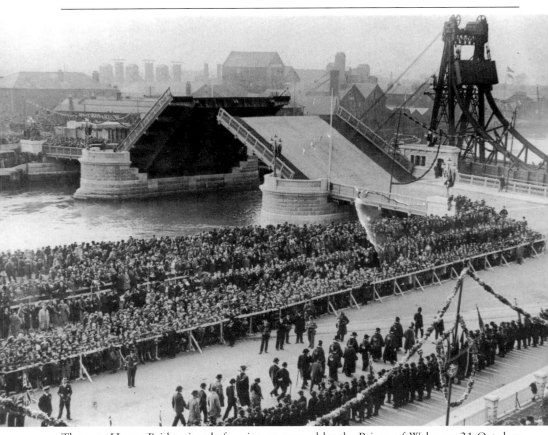

The new Haven Bridge, just before it was opened by the Prince of Wales on 21 October 1930. The temporary bridge, which was erected in 1928, is seen to the right of the new bridge. After inspecting the fishing fleet and lunching at the Town Hall, the Prince of Wales then proceeded by car over the temporary bridge to the west side, and after some speeches the prince declared the bridge open. The procession then crossed the new bridge and returned to the Town Hall.

Arnolds' horse and cart delivery service on Theatre Plain. The three attendants look very smart in their uniforms. Arnolds' must have had more than one of these carts, this being vehicle number two.

Brett's delivery van, decorated for a carnival in the 1920s.

A trolly or Yarmouth troll cart outside the old Town Hall, 1860s. Because Yarmouth had these exceptionally narrow rows, the inhabitants had to devise an original vehicle for transport, as no ordinary cart could enter them. These carts, modelled along the lines of the chariots of the Roman invaders, were about 12 ft long, with two wheels revolving on a box axle placed under the sledge, the total width of the vehicle being about 3 ft 6 in.

St Paul's Mission Room, Caister Road. This small church was moved from Stanley
Road. The windmill to the left was Greengrass Mill which stood on Hamilton Road,
formerly called Mill Road.

Old Yarmouth tramcar bodies in use as holiday chalets at Caister Holiday Camp,
1930s.

Delivering water, possibly in the very bad winter of 1947.

Returning from the Boer War, 1901. Millmount House is the large building in the background. The mortuary is seen on the corner of Row 45 and Mr Taylor's tobacconist's shop is seen with the sign outside.

SECTION NINE

Gorleston and Southtown

The Coliseum Picture Palace was erected on the site of the Fisher Institute in Gorleston High Street. The entrance was in the centre of the building, with two shops on each side. It opened to the public on 4 August 1913, with admission charges of 3*d*, 4*d* and 6*d*. The buildings were demolished in 1970. The shop to the right of the cinema was the Maypole Dairy.

The Two Bears Hotel in the 1860s. The building was rebuilt in 1910 when Mill Road was widened. There was an earlier Bear Inn at the foot of the bridge, and another public house on Southtown Road which had the name One Bear. Travelling wild beast shows were held at one time on a site nearby, so it is possible that the hotel derived its name from these fairs.

Southtown station opened in 1859. The photograph shows the inside of the station a few years after opening. It closed on 2 May 1970. It was then used by an oil company and demolished in 1977. Exhaust fumes now replace the smoke from the old steam engines, for the site today is a dual carriageway.

Bussey's grocer's shop, Gorleston High Street. Bussey's stores had been a feature of the High Street for many years. The photograph shows the shop just before it was demolished in 1968.

Sydney Weavers' dairy farm produce shop next to the library in Baker Street, 1940s. Here Mr Weavers is standing in the doorway of his shop with his three-wheeled delivery van outside. The shop has since been converted into a fish shop.

The horse tram station, Baker Street. This was situated to the rear of the later electric tramway station depot. The horse tramway opened on Good Friday, 1875. In 1900 it had ten trams and sixty-eight horses.

Local photographer Mr Yallop took this picture which shows the stretch from 94 High Street, looking towards the library. The two houses on the left can still be seen today, but are empty and boarded up, their fate as yet unknown. The shop with the man looking in the window is Mr Ball's newsagent's. The shop to the right was a baker's run by Mr Taylor. This shop and the one next door later became Clowes' stores.

Gorleston Library was opened in 1907 on Lowestoft Road. A feature of this building was its clock, which could be seen from Baker Street, High Street, Church Lane and Lowestoft Road. The library was demolished in 1975 and the present one built on the site.

Church Lane, looking towards Gorleston High Street, 1890s. The church gate can just be seen on the left. The only building in this photograph that still stands today is the last to the right.

Avondale Road, when both sides of the road were free from parked cars. Gorleston railway station is at the far end of the road. Open spaces on both sides of the road are yet to be built on.

The Suffolk public house, Pier Plain, Gorleston.

Mr Venables' chemist's shop, 118 High Street, c. 1906. By 1908 he had moved to Springfield Road. This shop later became the Co-op's first shop in the High Street.

The Old Commodore, one of the High Street's many public houses, 1920s.

Mr Newman's delivery van, about to depart on a family outing. Left to right: Ernie Newman with his brother John; the elegant-looking lady is Mrs Mapes; Aunt Harriet is sitting next to Mrs John Newman and her daughter May, who has her arm on the rear wing; far right is Mr Mapes.

A men only outing, just past the Halfway House on Southtown Road. Note the registration number, EX 750.

SECTION TEN

Wartime

During the Second World War Great Yarmouth suffered more bombing than any other coastal town. Today, little remains of the unique Yarmouth rows. Most of the slum clearance orders of the 1930s were no longer required. Conservation had not yet arrived. With the need to rehouse the population from war-torn areas, Yarmouth saw the complete rebuilding of streets such as Middlegate. From this aerial view of Middlegate Street and South Quay the bomb damage can be picked out. The line of the rows with a large open space in Middlegate Street around Row 92 is seen. This area was mainly destroyed in a terrible raid of April 1941.

Many well-known shops were destroyed in the raid of 7/8 April 1941. This is Kerridge's shop, King Street, the morning after the raid; it had to be demolished. Palmer's menswear shop is to the right.

Preparing for war in 1939 with the digging out for air-raid shelters on Church Plain. George Street is seen in the background, with the brewery to the left.

The hospital with sandbags in front to give some protection to the building. An ambulance is to the right.

Looking towards the Town Hall, Middlegate Street. The Tolhouse, also badly damaged in the April 1941 raid, is to the left, minus its roof. The building was further damaged in 1942, but was restored after the war and re-opened in 1961 as a museum.

The cellars of the larger buildings were used as air-raid shelters; the one shown is the working men's club in King Street.

Bomb damage to 88 George Street. Mr Darn's name is over the door. In the 1930s a fishmonger, Mr Hutchins, was the owner. This is another fine seventeenth-century building that in pre-war days stood proudly in George Street.

Digging out the basement for Marks & Spencer's new store in the early 1950s. Kerridge's shop has been demolished and the open space is seen opposite.

Acknowledgements

I am indebted to the many people who, over the years, have kindly lent me their photographs, which made possible both this book and the talks I give on Great Yarmouth.

I must thank the staff of the Reference Library, Great Yarmouth, especially Michael Bean and Stella Cordingley for their kind assistance over the years; Charles Lewis and John Read of Great Yarmouth Museum for their help and encouragement; Frank Bell and Peter Jones, with both of whom I have spent many a long winter's evening, discussing various photographs; Barry Daniels for allowing me to use his pictures; David Newman for permission to reproduce the front cover picture, and Mrs Cooke for her help; Mrs Joan Lobban for her assistance in correcting my bad grammar; finally Mrs Susanne Harvey, my fiancée, without whose great patience and encouragement this book would never have materialized.